Numeracy Pupil's Book
Year 1

Every effort has been made to trace copyright holders and to obtain their permission for the use of copyright material. The authors and publishers will gladly receive information enabling them to rectify any error or omission in subsequent editions.

First published 1999
Reprinted 2000

Letts Educational, Aldine Place,
London W12 8AW
Tel: (020) 8740 2270
Fax: (020) 8740 2280

Text © Peter Patilla and Paul Broadbent
Editorial, design and production © Gecko Limited, Bicester, Oxon
Illustrations © Peter and Janet Simmonett, except Beccy Blake: pp. 14, 52, 58;
David Pattison: pp. 8, 22; Peter Richardson: p. 17; Jake Tebbit: pp. 70, 80;
Andy Warrington: p. 20, additional graphics: Claire-Louise Simmonett.
Cover illustration © Beccy Blake.

British Library Cataloguing-in-Publication Data
A CIP record for this book is available from the British Library.

ISBN 1 84085 272 0
Printed and bound in Spain by Mateu Cromo
Letts Educational, a division of Granada Learning Limited. Part of the Granada Media Group

CONTENTS

Do you remember?

Write 3 numbers which are more than 10.

10

Estimate and check.

 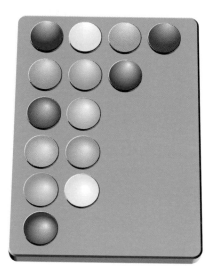 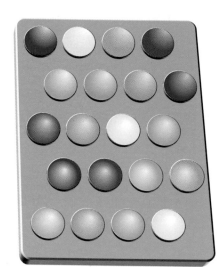

How many more to make 10?

Talk about coins.

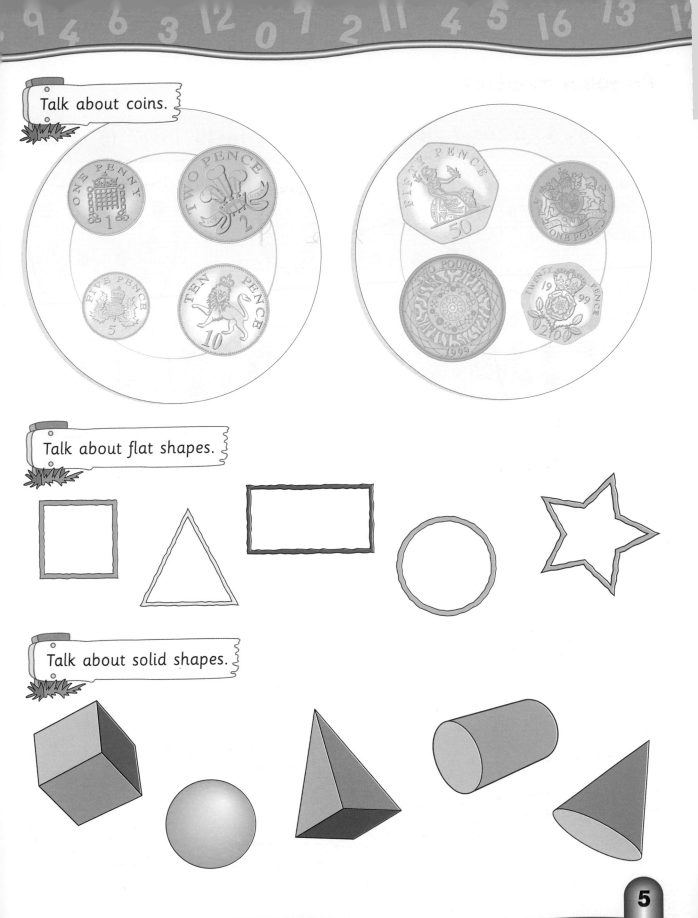

Talk about flat shapes.

Talk about solid shapes.

Counting

| 1 | 2 | 3 | 4 | 5 | 6 | 7 | 8 | 9 | 10 | 11 | 12 | 13 | 14 | 15 | 16 | 17 | 18 | 19 | 20 |

Count how many.

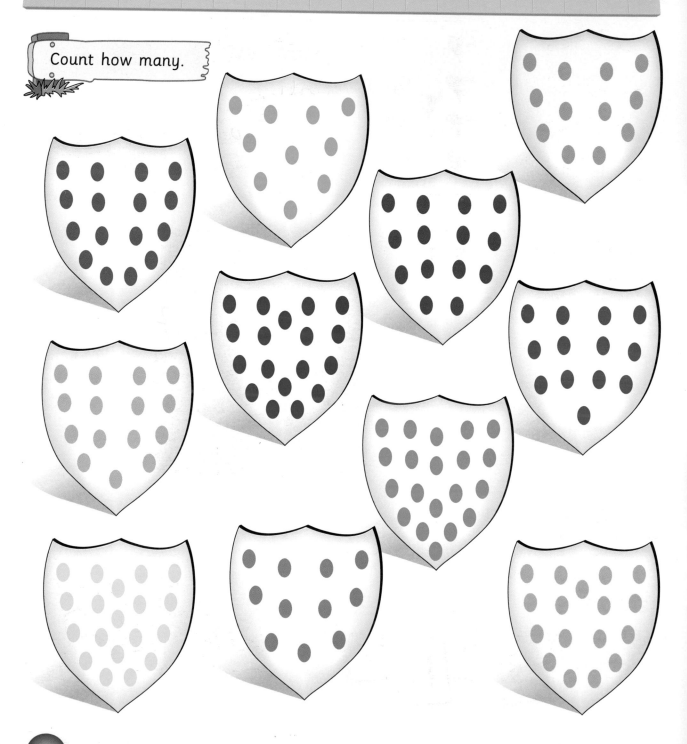

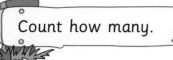

Count how many.

Which numbers are missing?

Challenge

Put these in order.

7

Place value

Which numbers are missing?

Write these numbers carefully.

1 4 7   0 3 6 8   2 9 5

Use counters.
Match answers to sums.

10 and 2

10 and 9

10 and 6

10 and 4

10 and 7

12   14   17   16   19

Challenge

Make some teens sticks.

13 is 10 and 3

Adding and taking away

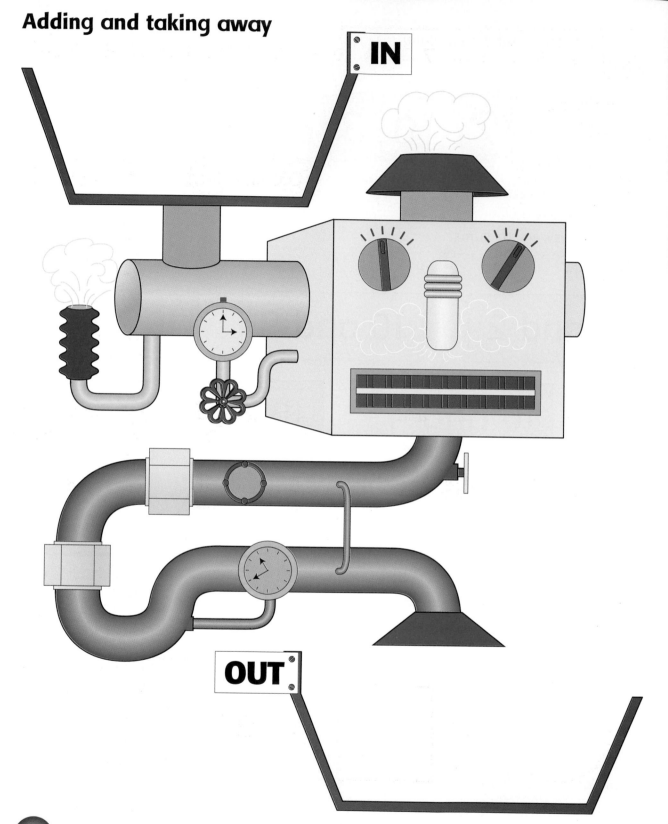

```
+--+--+--+--+--+--+--+--+--+--+--+--+--+--+--+--+--+--+--+--+
0  1  2  3  4  5  6  7  8  9  10 11 12 13 14 15 16 17 18 19 20
```

Add these.

3 and **2**   **4** and **4**   **2** and **8**   **5** and **3**

6 and **1**   **3** and **3**   **4** and **5**   **7** and **2**

Add these.

7 and **4**   **5** and **6**   **8** and **5**   **6** and **6**

8 and **7**   **9** and **6**   **8** and **8**   **6** and **7**

Challenge

Use counters.
How many can go in each shape?

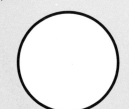 **−**  **=** **3**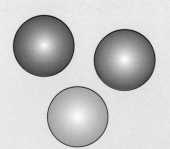

Solving problems

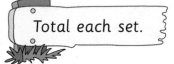

Total each set.

Match prices with coins.

8p

9p

5p

Challenge

Find different ways to make 10p.

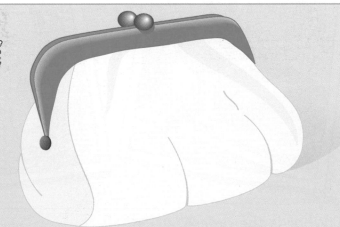

Measuring

What is the order?

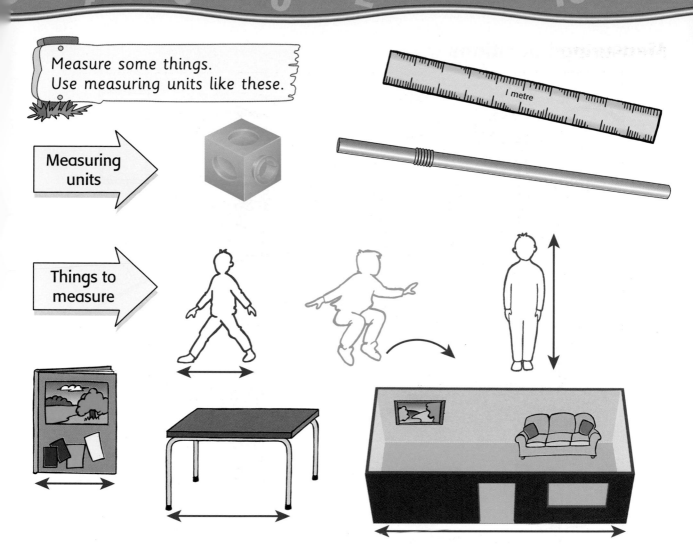

Measure some things.
Use measuring units like these.

I metre

Measuring units

Things to measure

Challenge

Make a picture ruler.

Measure with your ruler.

15

Shapes and positions

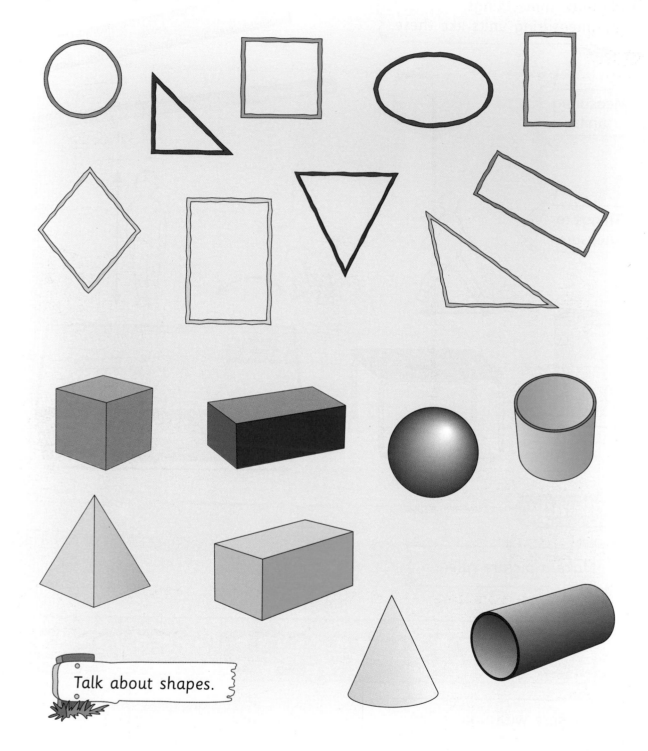

Talk about shapes.

What shapes are these objects?

Challenge

Make shape patterns.

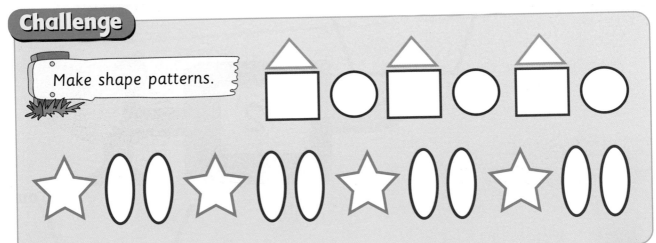

Review

Talk about these.

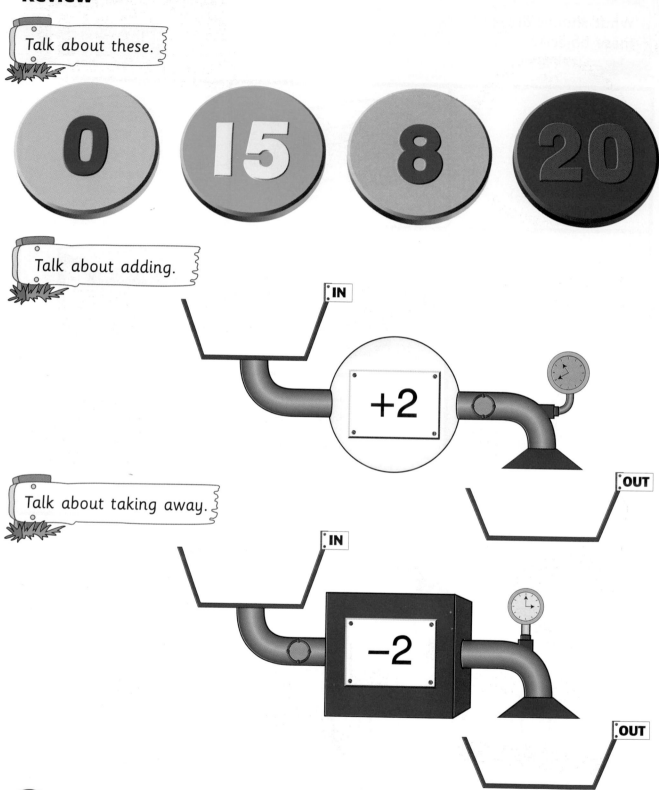

Talk about adding.

Talk about taking away.

Talk about time.

5:00

o'clock

Talk about shapes.

19

Counting patterns

Which numbers are missing?

What are the missing numbers?

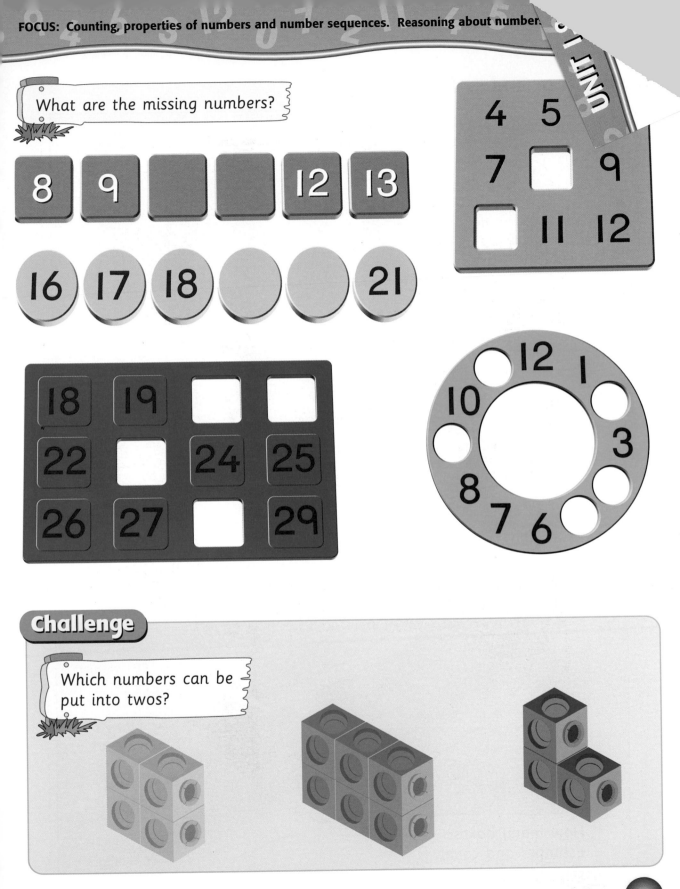

8 9 ☐ ☐ 12 13

4 5
7 ☐ 9
☐ 11 12

16 17 18 ☐ ☐ 21

18 19 ☐ ☐
22 ☐ 24 25
26 27 ☐ 29

12 1
10   3
8
7 6

Challenge

Which numbers can be put into twos?

Place value and ordering

How many boxes?
Estimate and count.

> What is 10 more than each of these?

> Talk about more, fewer, equal.

 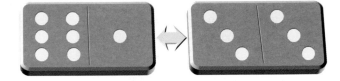

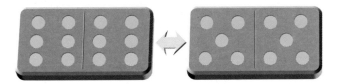 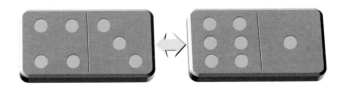

Challenge

> Hop in 2s.
> How can you reach 15?

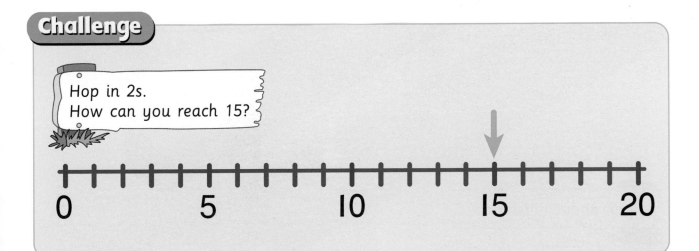

Difference

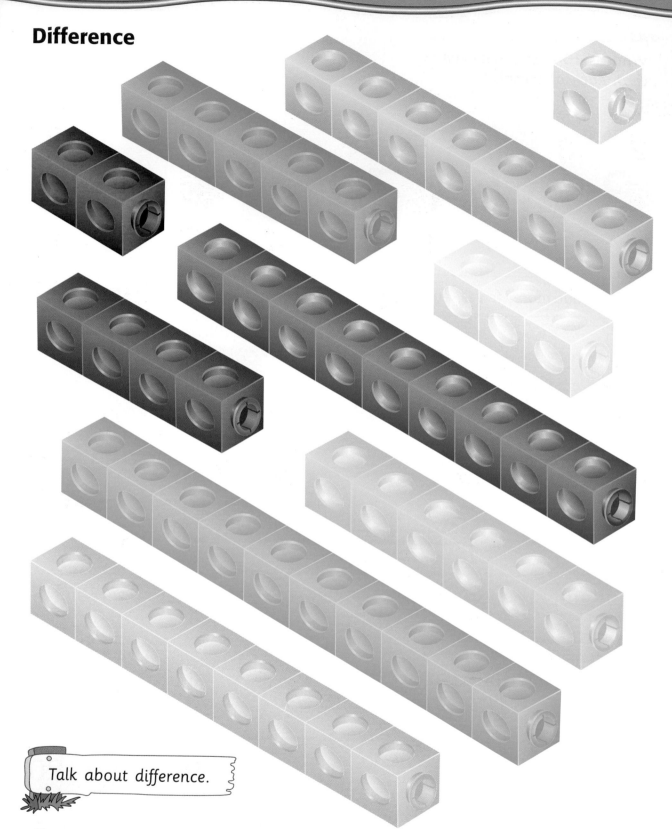

Talk about difference.

Write the difference between the coloured numbers.

| 2 | 3 | 4 | 5 | 6 | 7 | 8 | 9 | 10 |

| 4 | 5 | 6 | 7 | 8 | 9 | 10 | 11 | 12 |

| 7 | 8 | 9 | 10 | 11 | 12 | 13 | 14 | 15 |

| 13 | 14 | 15 | 16 | 17 | 18 | 19 | 20 |

Use a number line.
Where do you land?

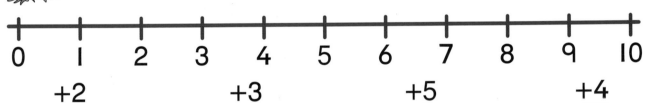

0 1 2 3 4 5 6 7 8 9 10

+2
3 →

+3
4 →

+5
1 →

+4
5 →

−1
9 →

−4
6 →

−5
5 →

−3
8 →

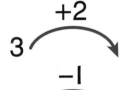

Challenge

Continue the pattern.

25

Money and problems

Write the change from 10p.

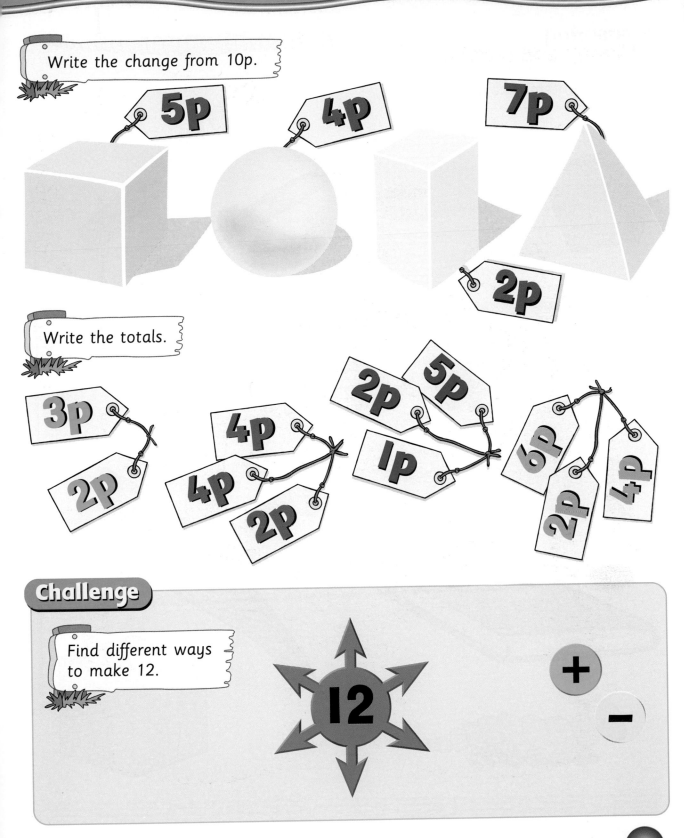

5p **4p** **7p** **2p**

Write the totals.

3p **2p** **4p** **4p** **2p** **2p** **5p** **1p** **6p** **2p** **4p**

Challenge

Find different ways to make 12.

12 **+** **−**

27

Measuring

Measure items like these.

Choose a measuring unit.
Measure some objects. Write a list.

	cubes
pencil	
table	
shoe	

	paper clips
span	
foot	
stride	

	straws
table	
shelf	
door	

Use the cubes to measure the lines.

Challenge

Measure right round some objects.
What will you use?

29

Information and time

Monday

Tuesday

Wednesday

Thursday

Friday

Saturday

Sunday

Talk about the weather.

What is the time?

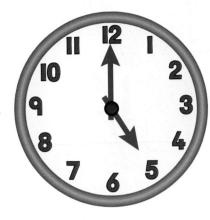

Challenge

Use a sand timer. Make a list of things you can do while the sand is running through.

Review

Write the number which follows each of these.

9   14   16   19   24

Write the number which is 10 more than each of these.

4   8   1   7   6

Add these numbers.

4 and 2   3 and 5   5 and 5

Take away 1.

4   3   6   7   10

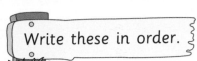
Write these in order.

5 8 3 7

14 9 10 7

Use the beads to measure the lines.

What is the time?

Do you remember?

Write the answers to these sums.

| 10 add 7 | 10 add 5 | 10 add 8 | 10 add 3 |

How much in each set?

Match the names to the shapes.

rectangle

circle

square

triangle

Match the names to the shapes.

| cuboid | cone | sphere | cube |

Add these.

Write the difference between
the coloured numbers.

| 1 | 2 | 3 | 4 | 5 | 6 | 7 | 8 | 9 | 10 |

| 1 | 2 | 3 | 4 | 5 | 6 | 7 | 8 | 9 | 10 |

Counting

Count in tens.

What are the missing numbers?

0	10	20	30			60
30	40			70	80	
80	70	60			30	20

Write numbers to 20 in twos.

0	2	4								20

How many hops to reach 20?

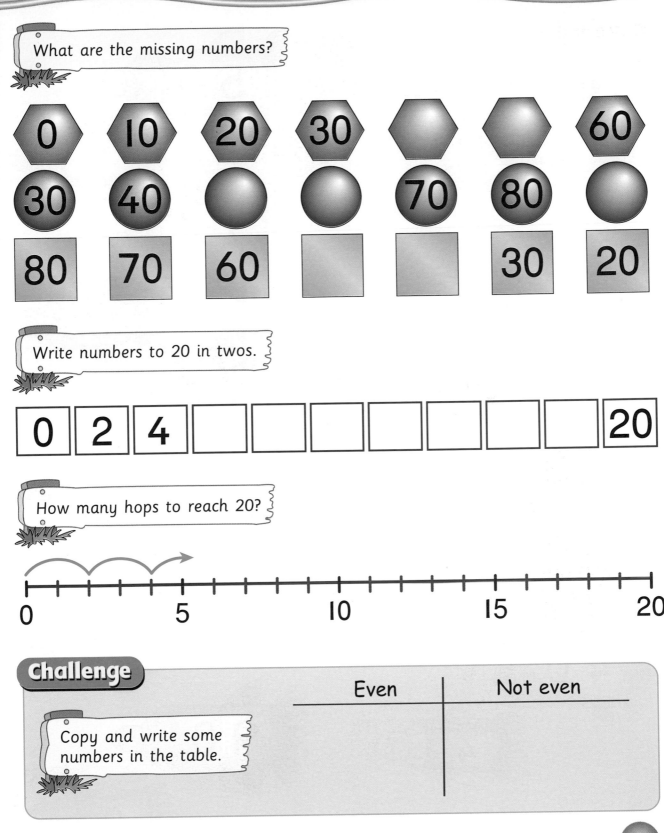

0   5   10   15   20

Challenge

Copy and write some numbers in the table.

Even	Not even

Place value

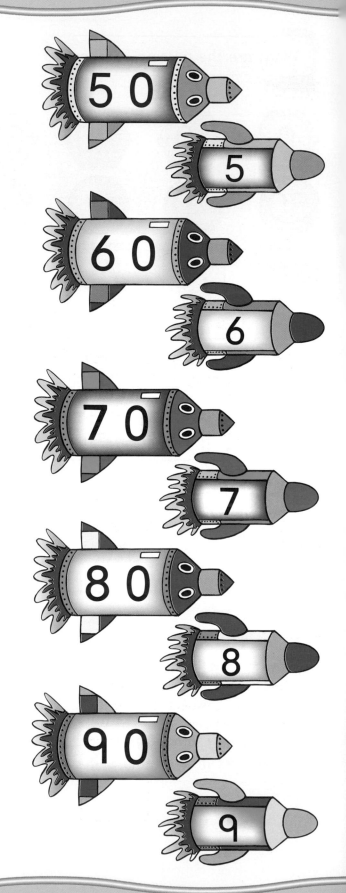

Copy and complete.

14 = 10 + ☐   23 = 20 + ☐   25 = 20 + ☐
31 = 30 + ☐   34 = 30 + ☐   47 = 40 + ☐

Copy and write the answer.

10 + 3 = ☐   10 + 7 = ☐   20 + 8 = ☐
20 + 6 = ☐   30 + 5 = ☐   40 + 2 = ☐

Talk about 10 more, 10 less.

14   12   17   13   19

Challenge

Place digits in the grid.
Which numbers can you make?

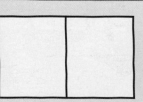

Adding and taking away

Corner numbers add up to 10.
Write the missing numbers.

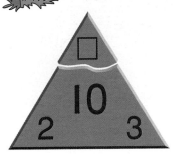

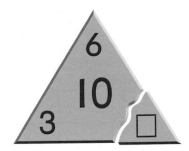

What is double each number?

Answer the sums.

7 – 2 =	5 – 5 =	3 – 1 =	6 – 0 =
4 – 3 =	9 – 3 =	8 – 2 =	10 – 4 =

Challenge

Use these numbers to make up some sums.

You can add and take away. You can use a number more than once in a sum.

41

Money

Talk about the prices of these items.

Total each purse.

Talk about fair swaps.

What is the change from 20p?

 **15p** **14p** **17p** **12p** **16p**

Challenge

You can add and take away.

Use 3 different coins.
Which totals are possible?

Balancing

Talk about heavy and light.

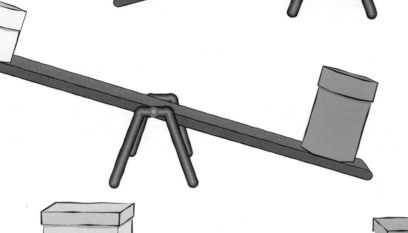

Talk about balances.

Choose some measuring units.
Weigh some objects.

Measuring units

Things to weigh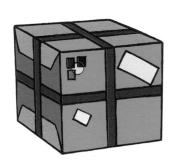

Challenge

Use 10 cubes.

Find:
3 heavier things
3 lighter things
1 thing about the same weight.

Shape and position

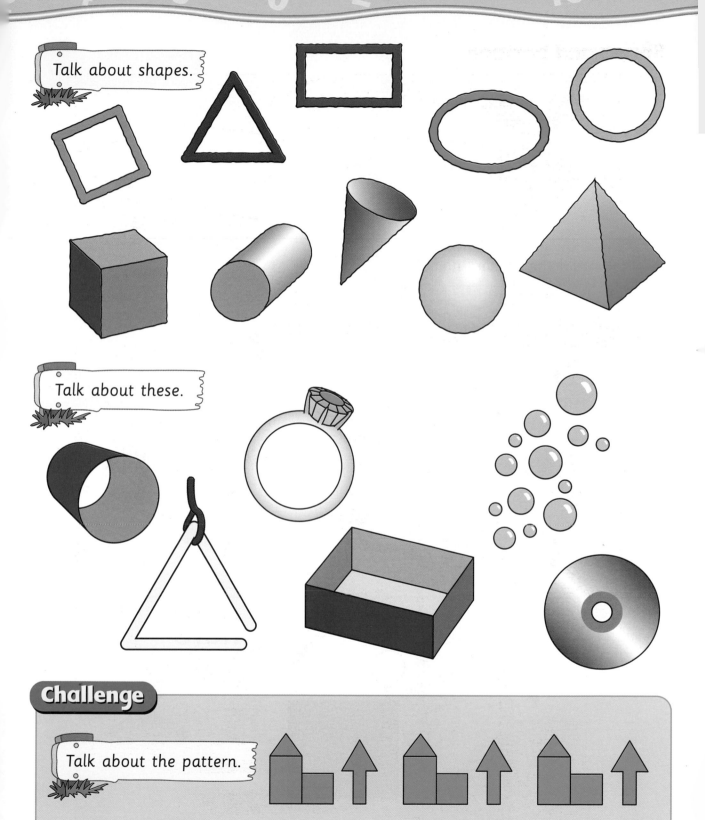

Talk about shapes.

Talk about these.

Challenge

Talk about the pattern.

Review

What are the missing numbers?

100 90 80 70

What could the missing number be?

40 50

Which numbers can be made?

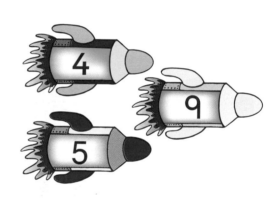

Talk about this.

10 less   10 more

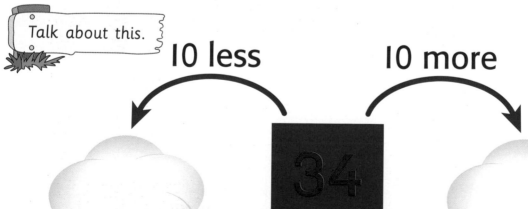

34

Answer the sums.

4 + 3 =	2 + 7 =	5 + 4 =	1 + 9 =
5 − 5 =	6 − 2 =	7 − 3 =	10 − 2 =

Talk about these.

Talk about these.

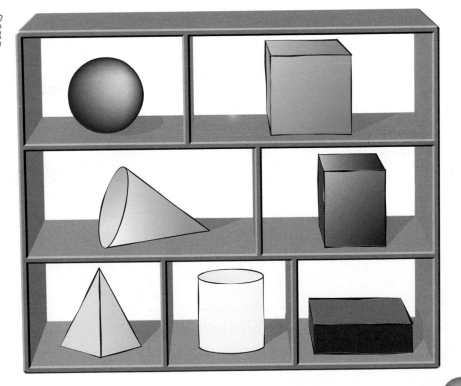

49

Counting patterns

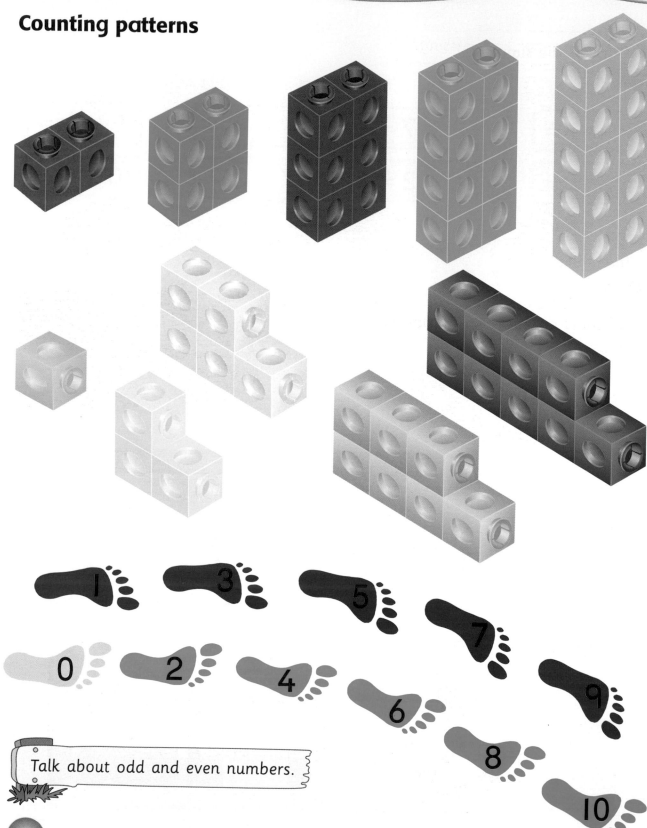

Talk about odd and even numbers.

Which numbers are missing?

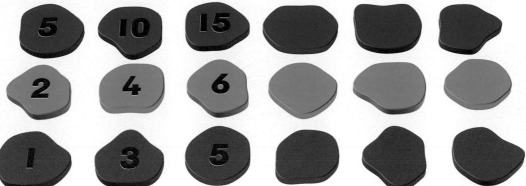

Draw dominoes. Make the total number of spots on each one an odd number.

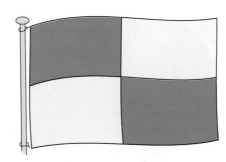

Draw flags. Use two colours. Make each one different.

Challenge

Use ① ② and ③.

Make each side total **5**.

51

Ordering numbers

Write these in order.

A B C D E F G H I J K L M
N O P Q R S T U V W X Y Z

What is the …   **5th letter?**   **9th letter?**   **15th letter?**   **last letter?**

Which position is …   **E?**   **H?**   **O?**   **W?**

Challenge

Use a 10p coin and other coins. Which amounts can you make?

Adding and subtracting

How many fingers?

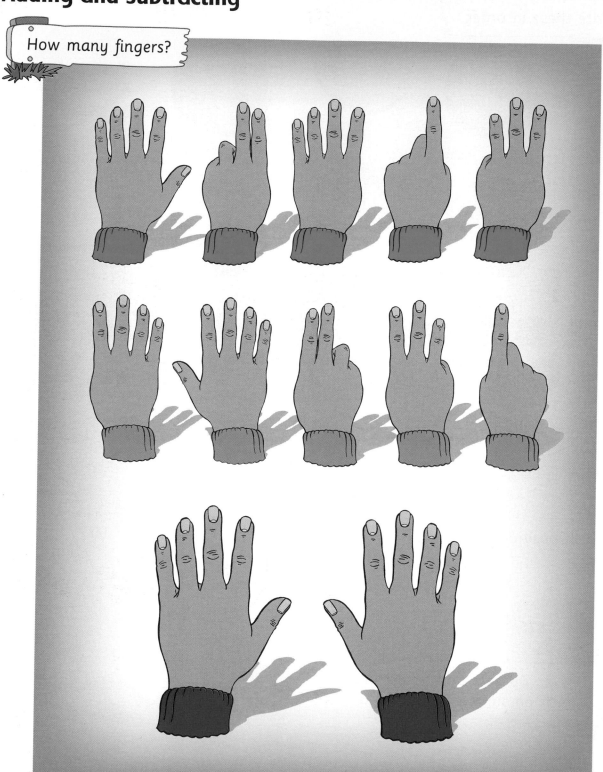

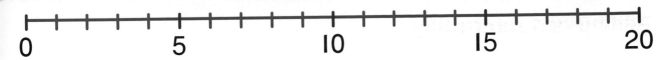

0   5   10   15   20

Answer the sums.

6 + 5 =	7 + 6 =	8 + 3 =	9 + 6 =
5 + 8 =	4 + 9 =	6 + 6 =	9 + 4 =

Total each set.

What is the change from 20p?

15p   12p   5p   9p

Challenge

Make up number stories.

3 + 5 = 8

☐ + 2 = 7

6 – ☐ = 2

55

Balancing

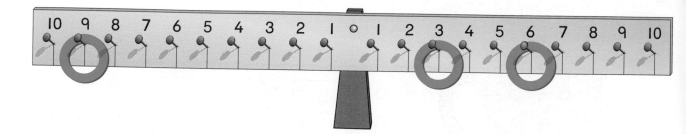

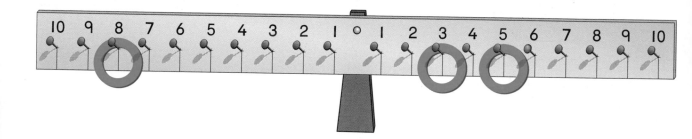

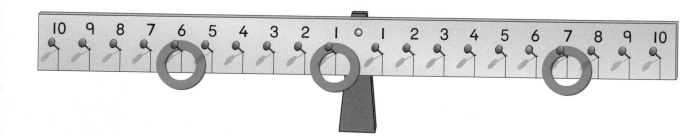

Talk about balancing numbers.

Weigh some objects like these. What units will you use to weigh them?

Answer the problems.

2 apples weigh ☐ cubes.

2 pears weigh ☐ cubes.

I apple and I pear weigh ☐ cubes.

Challenge

What will you use to weigh it?
Halve the ball. Make it balance.

Make a ball of plasticine.

57

Information

Talk about seasons.

Talk about the birthday chart.

May — David, Nicole
June — Diane, Ann, Ian, Jo
July — Omar, Laurel
Apr — Peter, Emily, Atul
Aug — Kelly, Alastair
Mar — James, Bethany
Sept — Emma, Fran
Feb — Thomas, Ashley
Oct — Sangita, Simon, Sue
Jan — Helena
Nov — Matthew
Dec

Challenge

Make a passport card.

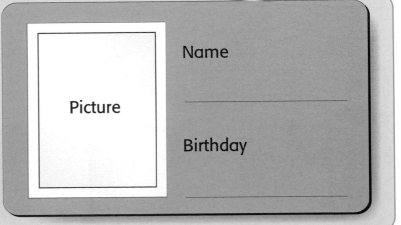

Picture

Name

_____

Birthday

_____

59

Review

Write 3 odd numbers.
Write 3 even numbers.

Which numbers are missing?

0   5   10   15

Estimate.

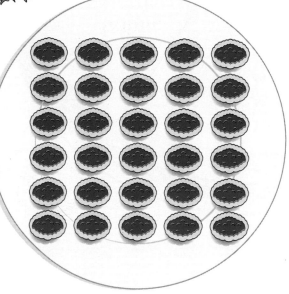 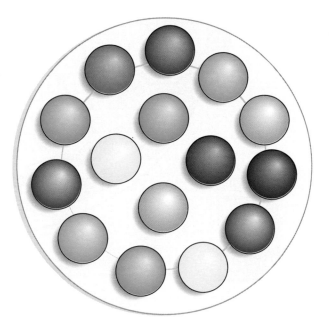

Write in order.

26   19   27   21

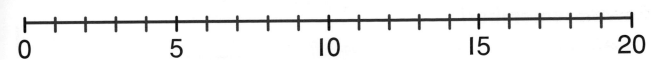

Answer these.

$$5 + 6 = \quad 4 + 9 = \quad 3 + 8 =$$

$$9 + 2 = \quad 7 + 6 = \quad 8 + 8 =$$

Total each set.

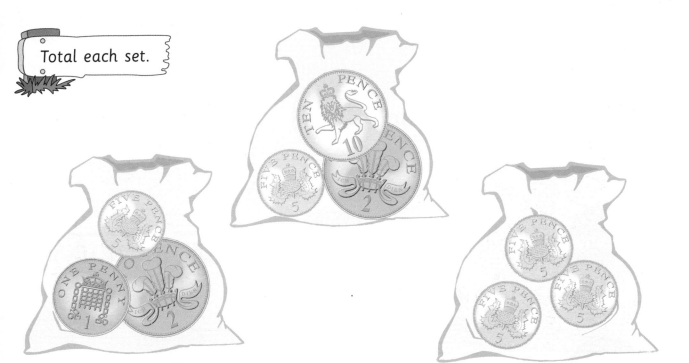

What is the change from 20p?

4p   9p   16p

Do you remember?

 17 is more than **19**   ⬚ TRUE ⬚ NOT TRUE

 15 is less than **20**   ⬚ TRUE ⬚ NOT TRUE

 16 is 10 more than **6**   ⬚ TRUE ⬚ NOT TRUE

 5 is 10 less than **20**   ⬚ TRUE ⬚ NOT TRUE

 4 is double **8**   ⬚ TRUE ⬚ NOT TRUE

 is more than   ⬚ TRUE ⬚ NOT TRUE

3 + 6 totals 9

| TRUE | NOT TRUE |

10 – 4 leaves 5

| TRUE | NOT TRUE |

 is a triangle

| TRUE | NOT TRUE |

 is a rectangle

| TRUE | NOT TRUE |

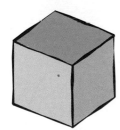 is a cube

| TRUE | NOT TRUE |

 is a cone

| TRUE | NOT TRUE |

Number patterns

Talk about counting in 5s.

Which numbers are missing?

2	4	6
1	3	5
5	10	15
14	13	12

Where do the numbers go?

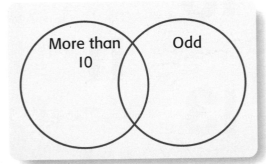

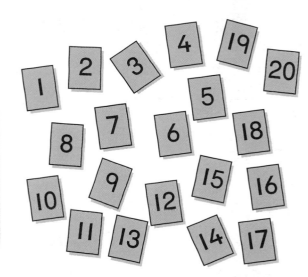

Challenge

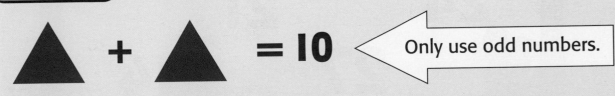

▲ + ▲ = 10 ◁ Only use odd numbers.

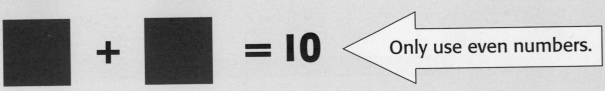

■ + ■ = 10 ◁ Only use even numbers.

Place value

Write 1 more than these.

 4 9 16 19 23 29

Write 1 less than these.

 14 10 20 17 30 26

Write 10 more than these.

4 6 8 14 16 19

Write 10 less than these.

 11 18 20 21 26 30

Challenge

These numbers are in order.
What could the missing numbers be?

 14 ? ? 20

Adding and subtracting

$$\boxed{} + \boxed{} = 10$$

$$10 - \boxed{} = \boxed{}$$

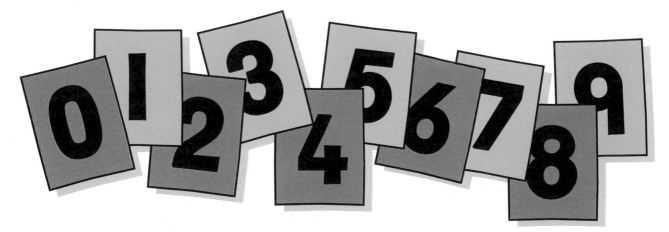

0   5   10

Answer these.

0
1
2
3
4
5
6
7
8
9
10

$5 + \square = 7$ $3 + \square = 10$ $2 + \square = 8$
$3 + \square = 4$ $6 + \square = 6$ $4 + \square = 5$

$\square + 4 = 5$ $\square + 2 = 7$ $\square + 0 = 6$
$\square + 3 = 10$ $\square + 1 = 9$ $\square + 3 = 6$

$4 - \square = 1$ $6 - \square = 2$ $5 - \square = 0$
$6 - \square = 4$ $10 - \square = 3$ $8 - \square = 8$

$\square - 2 = 4$ $\square - 1 = 5$ $\square - 6 = 2$
$\square - 3 = 5$ $\square - 4 = 4$ $\square - 1 = 9$

Challenge

What could the numbers be?

 − = **3**

Money

Talk about prices and money.

Total each set.

Look at these prices. How much change from 20p?

4p   5p   11p   15p   16p

Which coins match the prices?

18p   14p   16p   13p

Challenge

Match coins to the price labels.

How many different ways can you make a total of 10p?

1p   2p   3p   4p   5p   6p   7p   8p   9p   10p

Capacity

Talk about empty and full.

72

Choose some measuring units.
Fill some containers.

Measuring units

teaspoon   pot   jug

Things to fill

Challenge

Use plastic bottles. Put an elastic band
where you think half full is. Check.

Shapes and patterns

Use a mirror to complete each picture.

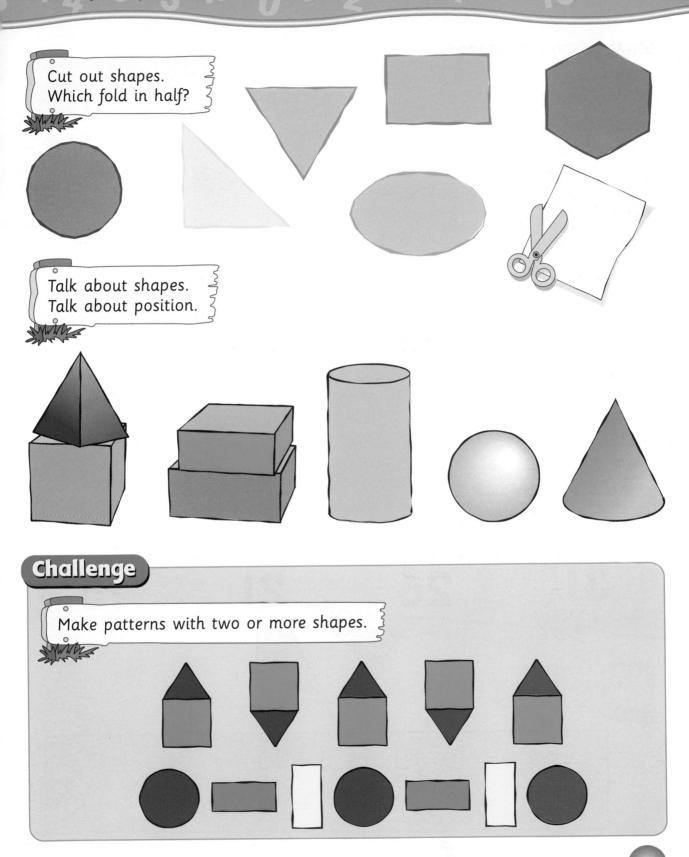

Cut out shapes.
Which fold in half?

Talk about shapes.
Talk about position.

Challenge

Make patterns with two or more shapes.

Review

Count in fives.

Count in odd numbers.
Count in even numbers.

What is 10 more than ...

8   **11**   **17**   **20**

What is 10 less than ...

31   **26**   **21**   **15**

Answer these.

$\square + 4 = 10$ $\square + 3 = 10$ $\square + 1 = 10$

$5 + \square = 10$ $8 + \square = 10$ $10 + \square = 10$

Answer these.

$\square - 3 = 4$ $\square - 2 = 4$ $\square - 5 = 4$

$6 - \square = 1$ $7 - \square = 1$ $9 - \square = 1$

Talk about coins.

Talk about these.

  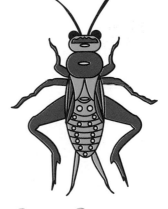

77

Counting patterns

Copy and carry on.

1	4	7	10
7	9	11	13
5	8	11	14

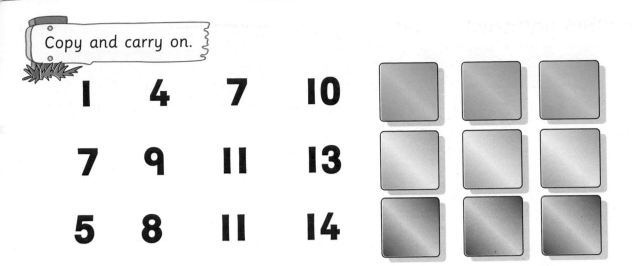

What do odd numbers end in?
Write some examples.

What do even numbers end in?
Write some examples.

Challenge

Which numbers could
go in ■ and ▲?

difference

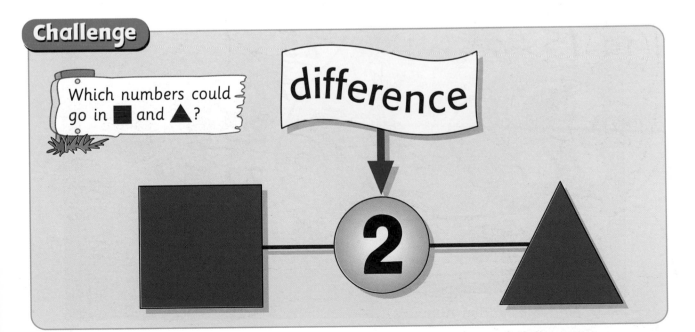

2

Numbers and calculations

Find the hidden numbers.

Write each row in order.

10   19   6   4

13   11   15   17

9   19   16   5

Total each set.

Answer these.

| 5 + 8 = | 4 + 9 = | 7 + 7 = | 6 + 8 = |

| 12 – 4 = | 16 – 8 = | 15 – 7 = | 11 – 6 = |

Challenge

Use the number track. Start on 0.
What size jumps land on 12?

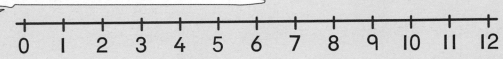

0 1 2 3 4 5 6 7 8 9 10 11 12

Mental calculations

0	1	2	3	4	5	6	7	8	9
10	11	12	13	14	15	16	17	18	19
20	21	22	23	24	25	26	27	28	29
30	31	32	33	34	35	36	37	38	39
40	41	42	43	44	45	46	47	48	49
50									

Copy and fill in the table.

In	1	3	4	7	9	10
Out						

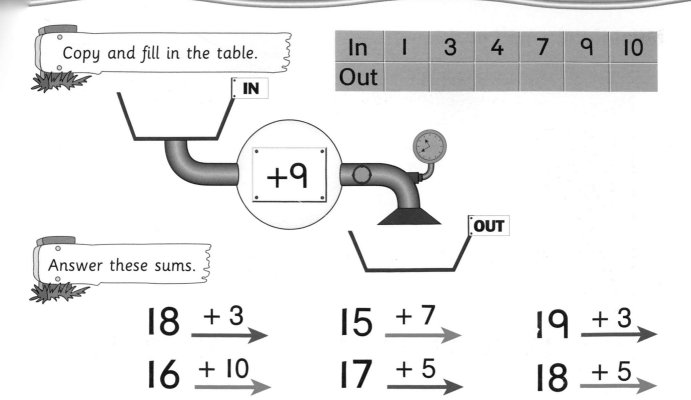

IN

+9

OUT

Answer these sums.

18 $\xrightarrow{+3}$

15 $\xrightarrow{+7}$

19 $\xrightarrow{+3}$

16 $\xrightarrow{+10}$

17 $\xrightarrow{+5}$

18 $\xrightarrow{+5}$

Solve these problems.

Lee has 8 coins.
Sue has half as many.
How many has Sue?

Sam has 6 stamps.
Nell has 10 stamps.
How many more has Nell?

Challenge

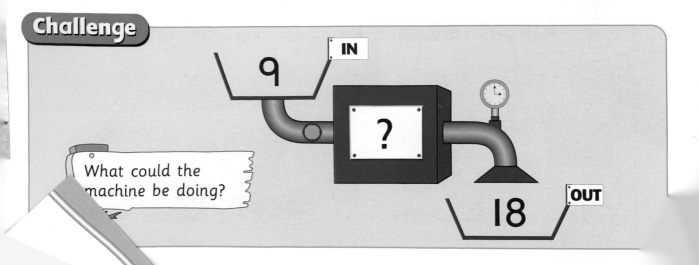

IN

9

?

OUT

18

What could the machine be doing?

Calculations and problems

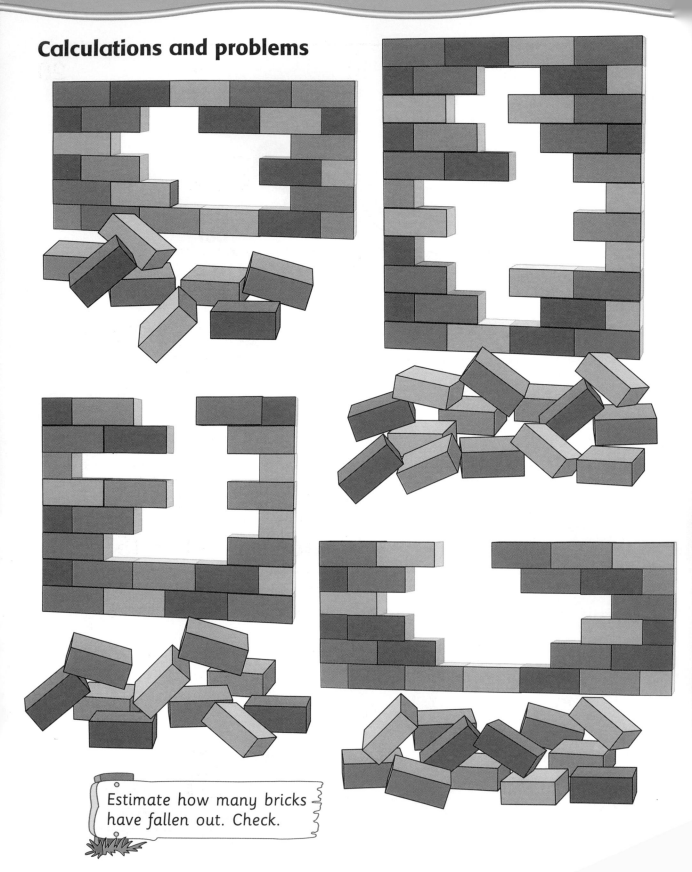

Estimate how many bricks have fallen out. Check.

0   5   10   15   20

Answer these.

$5 + 5 = \square$ $6 + 6 = \square$ $4 + 4 = \square$

$5 + 4 = \square$ $6 + 7 = \square$ $4 + 5 = \square$

$4 + \square = 13$ $5 + \square = 12$ $6 + \square = 11$

$9 + \square = 16$ $4 + \square = 15$ $8 + \square = 15$

$\square + 7 = 12$ $\square + 3 = 15$ $\square + 6 = 19$

$\square + 1 = 14$ $\square + 4 = 17$ $\square + 3 = 17$

$\square - 4 = 11$ $\square - 2 = 13$ $\square - 3 = 12$

$\square - 3 = 15$ $\square - 1 = 16$ $\square - 0 = 15$

$15 - \square = 12$ $16 - \square = 14$ $20 - \square = 16$

$17 - \square = 17$ $19 - \square = 12$ $18 - \square = 10$

Challenge

Write sums which have this answer.

5

Time

What time is it?

What are these times?

Talk about time.

Match the times.

Challenge

Estimate where 5 cupfuls will come to.
Use an elastic band to show the level. Check.

  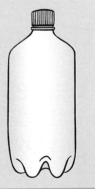

87

Information

bananas	I I I I I	5
oranges	I I I I I I I I	8
cherries	I I I I I	5
apples	I I I I I I	6
plums	I I I I I I I	7

bananas	🍌	🍌	🍌	🍌	🍌			
oranges	🍊	🍊	🍊	🍊	🍊	🍊	🍊	🍊
cherries	🍒	🍒	🍒	🍒	🍒			
apples	🍎	🍎	🍎	🍎	🍎	🍎		
plums	🫐	🫐	🫐	🫐	🫐	🫐	🫐	

How many ?

How many ?

How many ?

How many ?

How many bears altogether?

How many sheep?

How many cows?

How many horses?

How many pigs?

How many altogether?

Challenge

Show information about shoes in your class.

Review

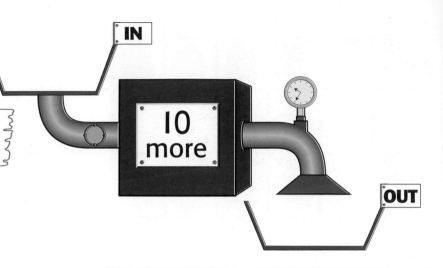

Add 10 more to 5 different odd numbers.

Copy and fill in the table.

In	3	5	10	15	19
Out					

Answer these.

$$\square + 4 = 10 \qquad 6 + \square = 20$$

$$10 - \triangle = 3 \qquad \triangle - 5 = 11$$

Talk about coins.

Talk about time.

03:30

Talk about shapes.

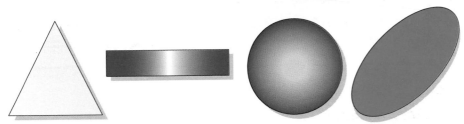

Talk about size and position.

Take away 9.

16   **17**   **14**   **21**

Numbers

0	zero		
1	one	eleven	11
2	two	twelve	12
3	three	thirteen	13
4	four	fourteen	14
5	five	fifteen	15
6	six	sixteen	16
7	seven	seventeen	17
8	eight	eighteen	18
9	nine	nineteen	19
10	ten	twenty	20

ten	10
twenty	20
thirty	30
forty	40
fifty	50
sixty	60
seventy	70
eighty	80
ninety	90
one hundred	100

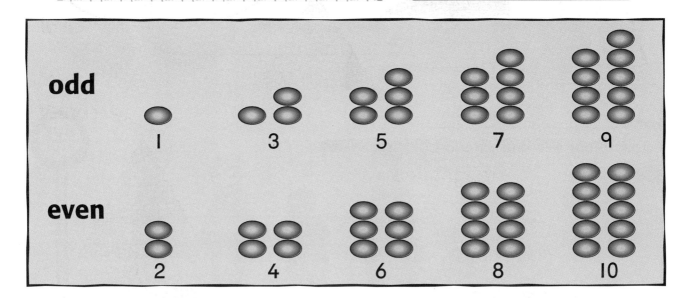

odd: 1 3 5 7 9

even: 2 4 6 8 10

These pairs total 10

10	0	7	3
9	1	6	4
8	2	5	5

Doubles

$0 + 0 = 0$ $3 + 3 = 6$

$1 + 1 = 2$ $4 + 4 = 8$

$2 + 2 = 4$ $5 + 5 = 10$

2-D shapes

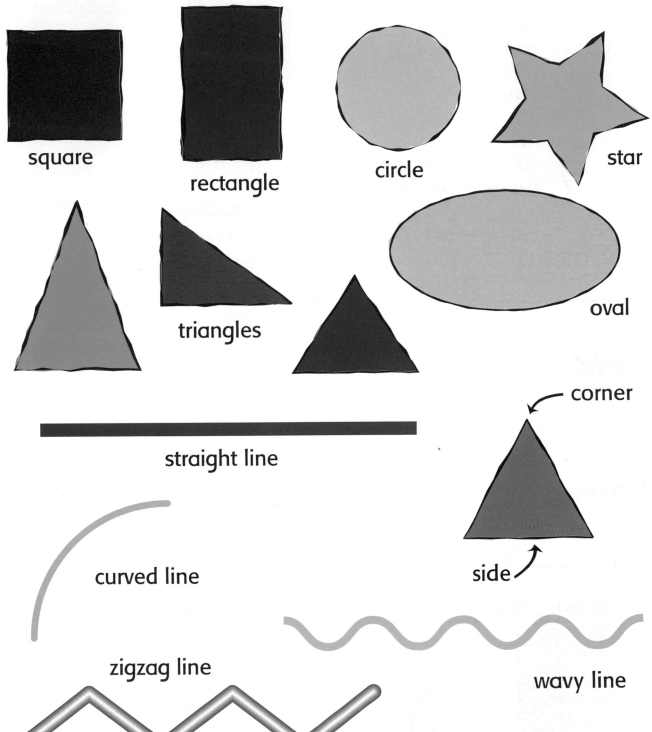

square

rectangle

circle

star

triangles

oval

straight line

corner

side

curved line

zigzag line

wavy line

3-D shapes

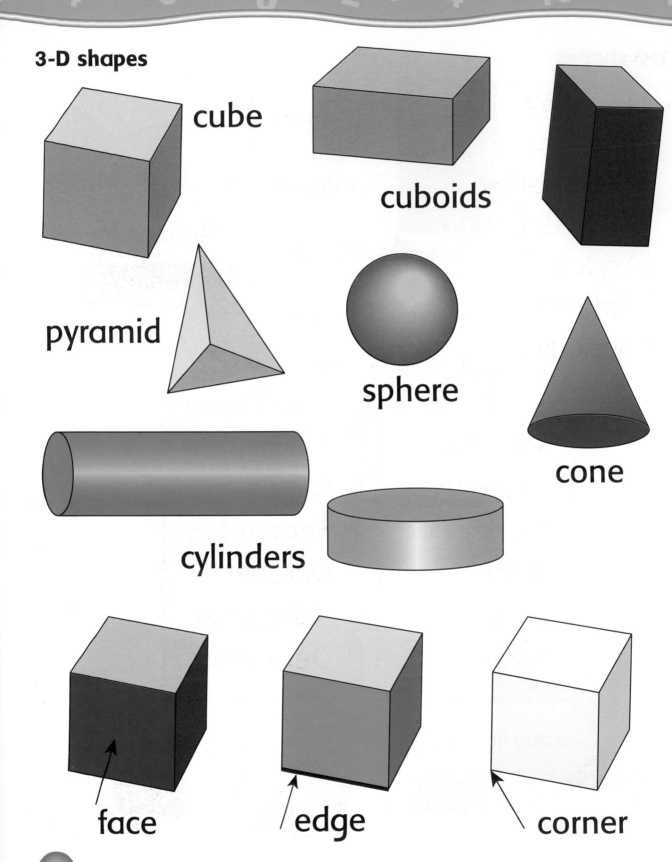

cube

cuboids

pyramid

sphere

cone

cylinders

face

edge

corner

Time

Monday
Tuesday
Wednesday
Thursday
Friday
Saturday
Sunday

Summer
Autumn
Winter
Spring

Morning
Afternoon
Evening

January
February
March
April
May
June

July
August
September
October
November
December

4 o'clock
4:00

half past 4
4:30

Do you remember?

Term 1 (pp. 4–5)

Estimate and check.

14   14   20

How many more to make 10?

$3 + 7 = 10$ $5 + 5 = 10$

$4 + 6 = 10$ $1 + 9 = 10$

Term 2 (pp. 34–35)

$10 + 7 = 17$ $10 + 5 = 15$

$10 + 8 = 18$ $10 + 3 = 13$

How much in each set?

$2p + 2p + 2p + 1p = 7p$

$2p + 2p + 1p + 1p = 6p$

$2p + 2p + 2p + 2p + 2p = 10p$

Match the names to the shapes.

 square   cube

 rectangle   sphere

 circle   cuboid

 triangle   cone

$4 + 3 = 7$ $2 + 5 = 7$ $3 + 3 + 1 = 7$

Write the difference between the coloured numbers.

The difference between 2 and 8 is 6.

The difference between 3 and 10 is 7.

Term 3 (pp. 62–63)

17 is more than 19	Not true
15 is less than 20	True
16 is 10 more than 6	True
5 is 10 less than 20	Not true
4 is double 8	Not true
50p is more than 20p	True
3 + 6 totals 9	True
10 – 4 leaves 5	Not true

 is a triangle   Not true

 is a rectangle   True

 is a cube   True

 is a cone   True